The Ashford Book of

Carding

A Handspinners Guide to Fibre Preparation

Jo Reeve

ISBN: 978-1-877427-00-8

Cover Design & Layout: Jo Reeve.
Printed in Malaysia through Willson Scott Publishing Limited.
Email: publish@willsonscott.biz, www.willsonscott.biz.

Acknowledgements

At the 2004 Creative Fibre Festival of the New Zealand Spinning, Weaving and Woolcrafts Society, I tutored a drum carding class with 15 wonderfully enthusiastic students. I wanted everyone to have their own drum carder but we were one short. Ashford Handicrafts had a stand in the trades hall and Richard Ashford came to the rescue, lending us one of their new machines. Everyone in the class wanted to use it! At the time, Richard mentioned the idea that a book about carding would be very useful, and so the seed was sown.

I would like to take this opportunity to thank Ashford Handicrafts for the opportunity to write this book, which I hope will inspire spinners to be creative with carding and above all, enjoy the process of transforming fibre into yarn.

Sincere thanks to Rowena Hart for getting me started and for her encouragement and invaluable professional guidance along the way.

I must also thank my husband, Daniel, for his support and advice throughout this project, and of course for planning and cooking the meals to keep our family fed as deadlines drew closer.

Contents

Colour

Projects

Introduction

Living here in New Zealand means it is almost impossible to avoid wool. Ever since I can remember, the ratio of sheep to people has been something like 5:1, just slightly in favour of our woolly friends!

My passion for wool began at the age of 6 when my grandmother introduced me to a pair of knitting needles and a ball of yarn I knitted my way through my childhood and teenage years, and then in my early twenties, came across a spinning wheel in a shop window. I was instantly attracted to the idea of creating my own yarn and within minutes had purchased an Ashford kitset Traveller. I wasted no time in getting home to assemble my exciting new possession.

That was over 23 years ago and at that time learning to spin went hand in hand with a fleece and a flick carder as there was very little in the way of commercial sliver available. Using hand carders was the next technique to master, and then, after some years, the opportunity to buy a drum carder came along.

Nowadays the range of good quality fibre available to spinners worldwide has broadened dramatically, and we are spoilt for choice - many breeds of fleece for any project, commercially carded sliver in natural or dyed colours, multi-coloured sliver, silk, angora, alpaca, mohair, cotton, and many others. Carding is the process that prepares these fibres for spinning. It is the first stage in the transformation from raw fibre to wonderful yarn and is a chance to exercise your creativity with magical mixes of fleece, colour and different fibres. There is nothing quite like the feeling of spinning from freshly carded fibre - so why not treat yourself!

I hope this book will not only be for the beginner, but will inspire more experienced spinners to get those carding tools out of the cupboard, dust them off and give them another go.

Carding

Carding

What is Carding?

Carding is the term given to untangling and opening up fibre in preparation for spinning. It can be done by hand (teasing) or by using one of three tools described in this book - a flick carder, double hand carders or a drum carder. Each tool has numerous rows of metal teeth that align fibres for spinning. The number of teeth per square inch can vary and is measured in points. The higher the point number, the more suitable for use with finer fibres.

Using these tools correctly, and in harmony with good quality fibre, means your carding will be relaxing and enjoyable. There is always a sense of satisfaction from carding by hand. It can feel almost ethereal as fibres are gently brushed or blended together in preparation for the next part of their journey - a unique yarn. Take your time with all methods of carding, choose your fibre carefully, and you will rewarded for your work.

The Tools

Flick Carder

For preparing individual staples of wool fleece for spinning, or teasing out for drum carding.

Hand Carders

Hard carders are used in pairs to prepare several staples of fleece at one time. They can also be used for colour and fibre blending using fleece and sliver. Hand carders produce a small rolag for spinning. Available in three sizes.

Mini
72 point and 108 point

Student
72 point

Standard
72 point and 108 point

Drum Carder

The drum carder is used for:

- Carding large quantities of fleece
- Colour blending
- Fibre blending

Available in 36 point for coarse fibre and 72 point for fine fibre.

Fibre Properties

Spinners love to experiment with different fibres. Luxury fibres such as silk, angora, mohair, alpaca and dog hair can be spun on their own or carded with each other or wool to create gorgeous blends - hand carded rolags or drum carded batts. They are a treat to spin.

If you are planning a blending project, being aware of fibre properties may influence the type of blend you choose.

Using different fibres means you can:

- tailor a blend for a particular purpose
- use up small amounts of fibre left over from projects
- make expensive luxury fibres go further
- add lustre
- add softness
- make a slippery or short fibre easier to spin

Here are the properties of some of the more popular fibres used by spinners:

Wool

Fleece wool from sheep grows in bundles called staples which vary in size between breeds. Staples have a regular wave pattern from end to end called crimp. The finer the wool, the closer the crimp spacing. Wool fibres are graded in microns by fibre diameter from fine to coarse. Some breeds have good lustre. Wool has elasticity which makes it durable and wrinkle resistant. It can absorb up to 30% of its own weight in moisture and not feel damp. It is available to spinners as raw fleece or washed and carded sliver or combed top. Wool fibres dye readily.

Mohair

Mohair fibre comes from angora goats and is long, white and lustrous. It is graded from fine to coarse, the fibres thickening as the animal grows. The finest fibre comes from the kid goat. Mohair is very strong, wrinkle resistant and dyes beautifully. It has less elasticity than wool.

Alpaca

Alpaca is a relative of the llama. There are two types: the Suri and the Huakaya. The Suri has long straight fibres which are silky and lustrous. The Huakaya has shorter fibres and a natural crimp. The fibre is graded by its fineness and measured in microns. Alpaca fibre is strong, warm and soft. It has less elasticity than wool, drapes well and can be dyed.

Silk

Silk is produced from the cocoons of silkworms. It is very fine and highly lustrous. Its fibre diameter is measured in microns. There are two types of silk readily available to spinners. Bombyx Mori is pure white and is produced from silkworms which have fed on Mulberry leaves. Tussah silk is a golden tan colour and comes from silkworms which have fed on Oak leaves. Silk is strong, resistant to pilling and has no elasticity. It is very soft and looks stunning when dyed.

Angora

Angora fibre comes from the angora rabbit. The fibres are very fine and very soft. They are straight, slippery and lack elasticity. Its fluffiness is created by the ends of the fibres working their way to the surface of a yarn or fabric. Angora fibre is less dense than other fibres therefore it takes a lot more angora to equal the weight of a small volume of fibres such as wool or mohair. Only a small proportion is required in a blend for its softness to be felt. Angora dyes well.

Cotton

Cotton comes from the cotton plant. It has very short fibres that range from 3/4 - 2 inches (2-5 cm) in length. It has little elasticity. Cotton has a soft handle, good drape and can be machine washed. Cotton takes dye well.

Dog Hair

Fine, soft fibre suitable for spinning comes from the undercoat of double-coated dog breeds. The outer coat of these breeds can be coarse and scratchy. The soft fibres from dog hair fluffs as it is worn, creating a fuzzy halo over a garment. It is water-repellant and therefore very warm.

Hair 1-2 inches (2.5 - 5 cm) long or longer can be spun by itself. The hair from most double coated breeds falls into this category. Hair shorter than 1 inch (2.5 cm) will shed a great deal if spun on its own. It is better blended with another fibre such as wool.

Flick Carding

A flick carder is a very handy little tool which will open up staples quickly and efficiently for spinning or preparing staples for drum carding. It can be used with washed or unwashed fibre. It's a good idea to get into the habit of preparing a reasonable quantity of staples to give you enough for a good spinning or drum carding session.

You will need a piece of leather, vinyl or other cloth to cover your lap and catch the dirt and debris which will fall out as you are carding.

Washed staples ready for flick carding

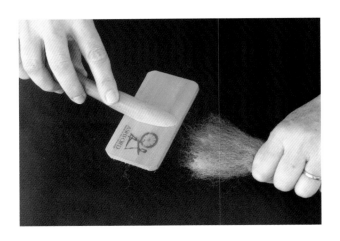

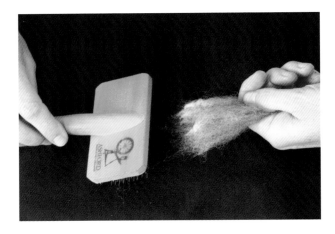

Step 1.
Hold the cut end of the staple in one hand (left hand if you are right-handed) and with this hand resting on your knee, gently 'bounce' the carder up and down on the tips. Try not to drag the carder through the staple.

Step 2.
Turn the staple over and card the other side.

Step 3.
Now hold the carded end and flick the cut end of the staple in the same way.

Step 4.
The staple should be free of dirt and all fibres separated from each other. It should look like a fan.

Store the carded staples in a suitable box - shoeboxes work well. Spin from either the cut end or the tip.

Carded staples ready for spinning

The flick carder is the ideal tool for effortless carding of the very long staples of Ashford's rainbow-dyed English Leicester fleece.

Rainbow-dyed English Leicester staples

Flick carded English Leicester staple

Unlike flick carding, which produces one staple of carded wool at a time, hand carding means you can process several staples of fleece at once to form a small rolag for spinning. You can use washed or unwashed fleece. You can also use your carders to make colour and fibre blends. For best results, tease out the fibres with your fingers before you begin.

Carding Fleece

One carder will hold the fibre while the other does the brushing.

Step 1

With one of the carders on your knee, place the teased staple lengths of fibre against the teeth at the handle end to catch it onto the carder, drawing down gently towards the top end as you let go.

Work your way across the carder filling it to the depth of the teeth. Over-filling the carder will make the fibre difficult to manage.

Filling the carder with staples of Corriedale fleece

Step 2

Hold the carder with the fibre in your left hand using an underhand grip - your fingers pointing towards your body. Hold the other carder in your right hand with an overhand grip and gently brush the fibre, at first just catching the tips of the staples. Continue brushing, gradually increasing the overlap until the carders overlap competely. The teeth should not be meshing together. At this stage about half of the fibre will be on each carder.

Brushing

Step 3

Position the left-hand carder in an upright position, still on your knee. With the teeth of the carders facing each other, place the top edge of the right-hand carder against the bottom edge of the left-hand carder. Make a swift movement up with the left carder which will now hold all the fibre. Repeat the brushing process. Again, there will be about half the fibre on each carder.

Transferring the fibre onto one carder

Step 4

Now the underside of what you have just carded needs to be done. Change the grip of your hands. Hold the right carder with an underhand grip and the left carder with an overhand grip.

Position the right-hand carder in an upright position on your knee and with the teeth of the carders facing each other, place the top edge of the left-hand carder against the bottom edge of the right-hand carder.

Changing grips to card the other side of the staples

Step 5

Make a swift movement up with the right-hand carder, pulling all the fibre off the left carder. The right carder will now hold all the fibre.

Brush again. Each carder once again holds about half the fibre.

Transferring the fibre to the right-hand carder

Step 6

Hold both the carders with an underhand grip with the teeth facing each other.

Make a swift, light movement up with one carder then a swift, light movement up with the other. All the fibre should now be sitting on top of one carder.

Getting ready to remove the fibre

Step 7

Roll the fibre from the top edge towards the bottom to remove it from the carder.

Rolling the fibre off the carder

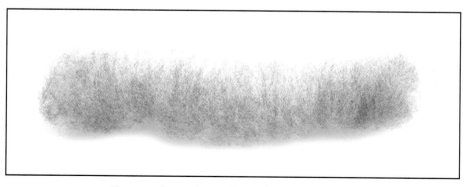

You now have the perfect rolag for spinning.

Colour Blending

Using the technique described for carding fleece, you can enjoy using colour on your hand carders. For these exercises, I used natural fleece with a variety of different fibres.

A natural brown Corriedale fleece and 'Nutmeg' Corriedale sliver.

A light coloured Romney fleece and 'Lime' Corriedale sliver .

Ashford's rainbow-dyed English Leicester with a light grey fleece makes a lovely rich blend.

Dark brown Romney and white Merino sliver go well together for a heathered look.

Different colour effects using coloured Corriedale or Merino sliver

Make a New Colour

Blue and yellow
make green

Yellow and red
make orange

A Striped or Heathered Look

Alternate colours across the carder.
Spin from the end of the rolag for a
stripey effect in the final yarn.

Place the colours in layers across the
carder. This will give a uniform blend
for a heathered look in the yarn.

Fibre Blending

Add a special touch to your hand carding by adding lustre or softness with luxury fibres.

These mohair staples have blended beautifully with 'Grape Jelly' merino. It is soft, fluffy and shiny.

The golden tan colour of tussah silk looks great with this 'Bean Sprout' Merino.

Sparkly 'Crystal Metallic' with black Merino for an evening garment.

Try this combination of Ashford Alpaca-Merino blend with dyed tussah silk. Very soft and shiny.

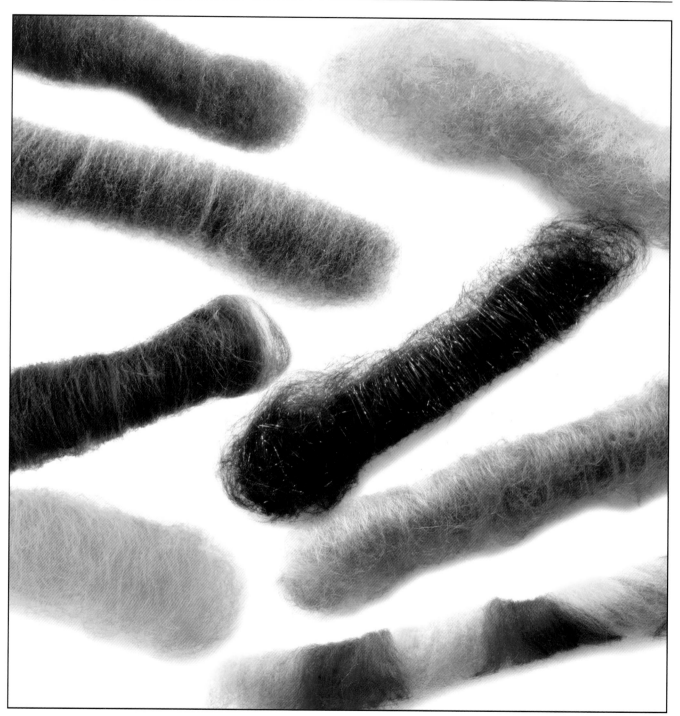

Drum Carding

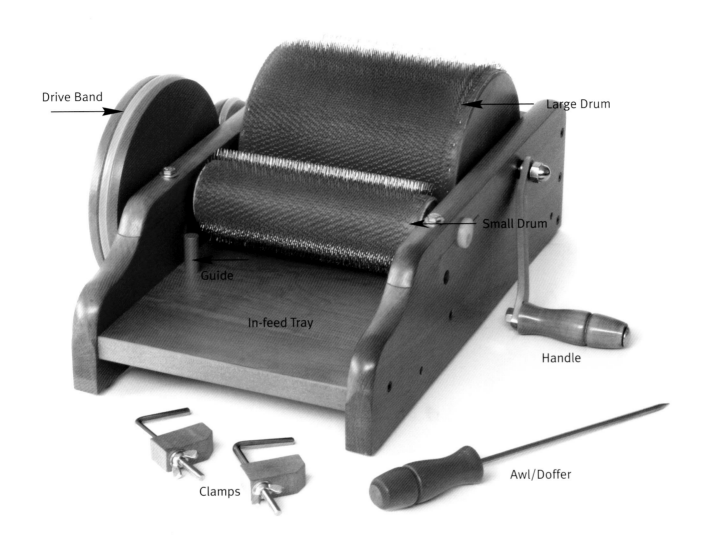

Drive Band

Large Drum

Small Drum

Guide

In-feed Tray

Handle

Clamps

Awl/Doffer

The Ashford Drum Carder

The drum carder is the ideal tool for preparing large amounts of fibre for spinning. You can use your carder to make beautiful batts from natural coloured fleece, be creative with colour and fibre blends using commercially prepared sliver, or a combination of both. There are many other good reasons for using a drum carder:

- You have the versatility to create just what you want from multi-coloured sliver to luxurious blends of wool and silk
- You can expand leftovers from other projects into a range of interesting blends
- You can make consistent colour and fibre blends
- Short and slippery fibres can be blended with longer fibres to make spinning easier
- Patchiness in dyeing is usually dispersed in the carding process
- You can process larger quantities of fibre than you could with a pair of hand carders
- Many colours can be processed in several ways
- Drum carded batts are really easy to spin as they are open and airy

Choosing a Drum Carder

It is important to use the appropriate carding cloth for the type of fibre you intend carding. Fine teeth (72 pt) are suitable for carding the finer breeds of wool such as Merino and Corriedale and for blending short fibres such as angora and cotton. Thicker teeth (36 pt) are suitable for coarser and stronger fibres.

Care of Your Drum Carder

To clean the carding cloth, you can use a stiff brush or flick carder. The bristles need to be at least as long as the teeth on the carder otherwise it cannot reach the base of the cloth and will not remove all the fibre. Push the brush or flick carder right down to the base of the teeth to ensure all fibres are removed. Clean your carder in a really good light, sunlight is perfect. Work your way around the small drum, then the large drum. You will need to go around more than once to ensure both drums are completely clean.

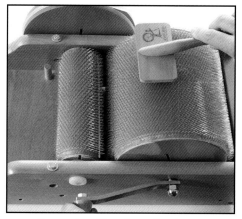

Your Ashford drum carder comes complete with an awl (sometimes called doffer) for removing the carded batt. Do not use the awl for cleaning the carding cloth. It will damage the cloth and bend the metal teeth out of alignment.

Removing fibre from the large drum with a flick carder

Oil your machine regularly according to the instructions which accompany your carder.

The distance between the two drums is pre-set in the factory so that the teeth are not quite touching. I recommend the drums be set slightly further apart so that a credit card can just slide into the gap. This enables me to card a wide range of fibre without the need to adjust the drums. All the exercises in this book were carded on this setting.

Occasionally the drive band may come off if fibre gets caught around the pulleys. Replace the drive band as follows:

 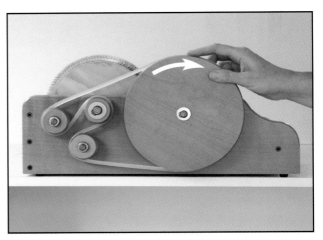

Replacing the drive band

Turning the drive wheel to 'snap' the drive band into positiion

Using the Carder

Clamp the drum carder to the table when in use to prevent it from sliding around the table. This frees up both hands and allows you to do the job efficiently. Before using the carder, check that both drums are free of all fibre. This is particulary important when changing from one colour to another. All fibre needs to be opened up before you feed it onto the carder. You should be able to see the infeed tray through the teased fibre.

Fleece: It will be kinder on your machine to card fibre that is clean, free of vegetation and well teased. It will not remove dirt, thistles, short cuts, lumps or noils - it will only distribute them through the entire batt. It is no fun to be picking them out as you are spinning. When carding fleece I like to give the tips a quick flick with the flick carder and then tease the other fibres open with my fingers. This ensures there are no clumps in my carded batt.

I like to wash my fleece in bundles of about 6 ounces (170 grams). This gives me a reasonable amount of fibre for carding and spinning. Place the staples in a plastic basket or mesh bag with the tips facing in the same direction. This helps with separating the staples once they are washed and dried. Submerge the basket or bag into a tub of hot, soapy water using about 5 tablespoons of a mild washing powder or pure soap flakes.

Staples ready for washing

Submerging the basket into hot, soapy water

Let the staples soak for about an hour, drain the tub and gently press the staples to remove excess water. Repeat the wash once more. Rinse in warm water three times or until the water is clear. Remove the staples, wrap in a towel and remove excess water by using the spin cycle on your washing machine. Remove from the machine and lay out flat to dry.

Commercial Sliver: Commercial slivers are usually packed fairly firmly into bags after carding and can become compacted. They are usually too thick to feed directly onto the carder and will put a strain on your machine and possibly tear the fibres. Peeling a strip off the side of the sliver assists greatly with opening up the fibres and gives you a manageable amount to work with. Gently pull on the strip to lengthen it a little, but not so much that it drifts apart, and spread it out widthwise.

Fleece to Sliver

Place your well-teased staples onto the infeed tray and turn the handle **slowly and steadily.** Feed the staples in with your left hand as your right hand turns the handle in a clockwise direction. Keep the fibre between the guides, away from the edges of the drum, to avoid it being drawn around the axles. Do not hold onto the fibre as you feed it in. If the fibre supply doubles back on itself, stop turning the drum, draw out the fibre a little and continue carding.

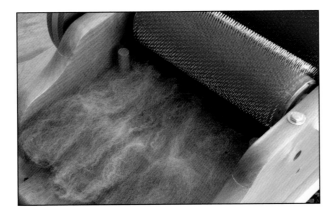

Feed the fibre on like this

Not *like this*

There should be little or no fibre accumulating on the small drum. If there is, then you may be feeding on too much fibre at once or feeding it on too fast. Try and resist the temptation to load as much as possible onto the drum. It is more efficient to process several small batches rather than one or two large ones.

If some fibres do get caught on the small drum, stop carding when the seam of the carding cloth on the small drum is showing and using your awl, slide it under the fibre along the metal strip. Lift the fibres up and onto the big drum. Continue carding.

Feed on enough fibre to fill the large drum. As a rule of thumb, I consider the drum 'full' when I can just see the carding cloth and doffing strip through the fibre. This gives me a manageable sized batt for removing from the carder and drawing out into a sliver for spinning.

Removing the batt:

Position the doffing strip of the main drum so it is on top. Slide the awl under the fibre about half way along the metal strip and gently lift the fibres up until they separate. Continue along the remaining half. Make sure the batt is separated all the way across otherwise it won't peel cleanly off the drum.

Separating the fibre along the doffing strip

Now gather up the ends of the fibre and pull down over the back beam with a small amount of tension. The drum will turn freely in the opposite direction to carding and the batt should peel away cleanly from the carding cloth.

Peeling the batt off the drum

Divide the batt in half down its length. Draw each half out lengthwise then spread out to the width of the infeed tray and card each piece again. Remove the batt and hold it up to the light. If the fibres look evenly distributed and there are no clumpy looking areas, then it is done. Otherwise, divide it in two and pass it through again.

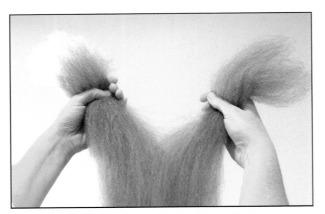

Splitting the batt in half lengthwise

Carding the batt a second time

Preparing your batt for spinning

To spin your beautiful batt, you will need to pull it lengthwise into a sliver. Roll it up widthwise, then holding it firmly with your hands about 10-12 inches (25-30 cm) apart, gently pull until the fibres start to move. If you pull too hard it will drift apart. Move one hand to where the fibre moved and the other about the same distance apart as they were before and pull again. Work your way up and down the sliver until it is as thin as you prefer for spinning. If the fibre won't move easily when you start pulling, place your hands further apart.

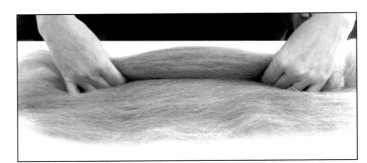

Rolling the batt widthwise

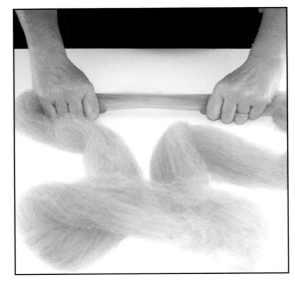

Pulling the batt into a sliver

Skein of handspun Corriedale wool

Colour Blending

Fibre can be arranged in several ways on the drum carder to achieve different effects with colour in your spinning. Use washed and dyed staples or commercial sliver. If you are using dyed fleece, card each colour separately before you begin blending. In this section I have used coloured slivers from the Ashford Corriedale and Merino ranges.

Blending Colours Side-by-Side

This technique makes a multi-coloured sliver. Take a 12 inch (30 cm) length of sliver and peel a thin strip off the side. Draw it out a little lengthwise and feed each colour separately onto the carder, placing them side by side. The wider each strip of colour, the brighter and clearer it will be in the finished yarn. Compare the three blends below of three, six and nine colours. Turquoise has been used in each one but it is much brighter in the yarn with three colours than in the yarn with nine colours. The yarn is 2-ply.

Three Colours

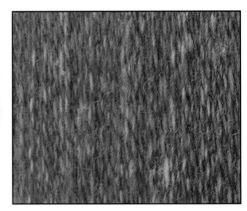

Six Colours

Nine Colours

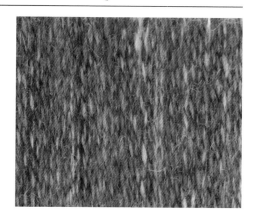

Remove the batt and pull into a sliver as shown on page 31. There are two effects you can achieve in the yarn from this method of carding:

An Evenly Coloured Yarn

All the colours in the batt need to be kept together along the entire length of the sliver. You will need to take your time with this. Turn the fibre over regularly as you proceed, to check that all the colours are still present. It is a lot easier to do this with a thin batt.

Slow down your spinning so you have time to control the fibre supply and keep all the colours in the drafting triangle.

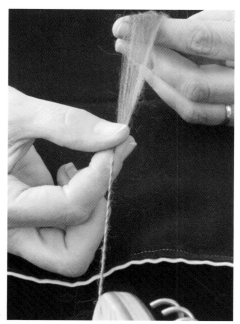

Spinning 3 colours that were placed side-by-side on the carder

A Stripey Yarn

You can be a little more relaxed about how you make your sliver. If the colours come and go along its length, you will have an interesting stripey look to your yarn.

Blending Colours in Layers

This technique makes a heathered or flecked yarn or a completely new colour. Be careful with this method that you don't overblend and end up with dull colours. Keep in mind that the spinning and plying process will blend the colours a little more.

Peel off a section of your sliver, spread it out widthwise and feed onto the carder, filling the width of the drum. Repeat with each colour. After the first pass, divide the batt in half lengthwise, spread each half out to the width of the drum and card again. Keep dividing the batt and carding until the colours are blended to your liking.

Tangerine   *Turquoise*   *Magenta*

Layers on the drum after the first pass

Layered batt after one pass through the carder

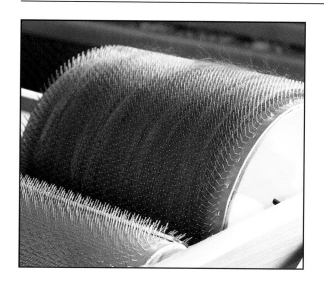

Two passes

Three passes

Making a Self-striping Yarn

This technique is ideal for preparing a self-striping yarn for smaller knitted items such as socks, gloves, mittens and scarves. The frequent colour change along the length of the batt results in spun yarn that creates short stripes in knitting. The stripes are sandwiched between two thin layers of one colour.

The number of stripes you can fit around the drum will depend on the staple length of the fibre you use and how much you overlap them. You can use a different colour for each stripe, alternate two colours or have a rotating sequence of lots of colours. The length of each stripe in the yarn will depend on how much fibre you place on the drum and how many times you divide the batt into strips.

Feeding on a thin layer of one colour

Step 1

Feed a very thin layer of one colour across the width of the drum. In this example I used green.

Step 2

Place the first stripe of colour as follows:

Pull off a strip of coloured sliver and divide it into 6 inch (15 cm) lengths. Take one portion and place it directly onto the main drum by holding it down with the palm of your right hand. Gently pull the fibre away with your left hand to leave a staple-length on the drum. Work your way across the width of the drum as evenly as possible.

To make the next stripe, turn the drum a little and load another colour in the same way. Overlap the colours to make the batt stronger. Continue around the drum until you meet up with the first colour.

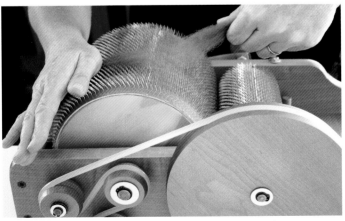

Placing the first stripe onto the main drum

If the drum wants to rotate freely, you may need to press your body against the handle to secure it in the required position.

Step 3

Feed on another thin layer as you did in Step 1. The stripes are now sandwiched between the two thin layers.

Step 4

Carefully remove the batt from the carder. It should look like this. I used three colours to make six stripes, two stripes for each colour.

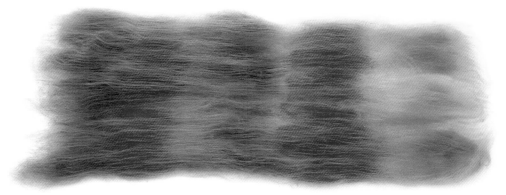

The 6 stripes sandwiched between the two thin layers

Step 5

Divide the batt lengthwise into two strips, pulling each one out in length a little in preparation for spinning. I spun a medium 2-ply yarn and finer navajo plied yarn to show the completely different effects you can achieve.

2-ply yarn

Navajo plied yarn

Blending Different Fibres

The comment I hear most from spinners when blending fibres on the drum carder is, 'it keeps collecting on the small drum". There are several reasons for this - the fibres are too short, the fibres are too fine for the carding cloth or too much fibre is being fed on too quickly. Not only is this frustrating but much time and money can be wasted. You can successfully card these short, fine "luxury" fibres by blending them with wool. Instead of being caught on the small drum, the luxury fibres are assisted onto the big drum by the longer wool fibres.

Wool batts should be thoroughly carded first. Because another layer is being added, it is easier to work with thin batts.

Step 1

Spread the wool batt out lengthwise a little and then widthwise until it is about twice the width of the carder.

Tease open the luxury fibre and spread it evenly over half the width of the wool batt.

Dyed silk being added to white Merino

Step 2

Fold the remaining half of the batt over onto the luxury fibre, encasing it between two layers of wool.

Feed the folded batt onto the carder, turning the crank very slowly and steadily. If the fibre supply buckles, it is too thick. Stop turning the drum, pull out the batt a little then continue carding. Do not hold onto the fibre as it goes into the carder.

The folded wool batt with silk between the two layers

Step 3

Remove the batt and divide it in half lengthwise. Spread each half out to the width of the drum and card again. Blending different fibres takes a little more work than blending colours and you may need to make 3 or 4 passes for a thorough blend.

The proportion of each fibre you use in a blend will affect the appearance and handle of the final yarn. For example, there needs to be a high proportion of silk in a blend to show off its lustrous quality whereas only a small proportion of angora is needed for its softness to be felt.

Luxury fibres are more expensive than wool so take some time to carefully plan your project and think about what qualities you want in your final yarn (refer to the "Fibre Properties" section).

The blend on the previous page is 20% silk and 80% Merino wool. Although it is very soft, the sheen of the silk has been lost because of the high proportion of wool used.

Use at least 50% silk in a wool/silk blend for its lustre to show.

20% silk/80% Merino blend

50% Silk/50% Wool

This blend was passed through the carder 4 times. It has a wonderful soft feel and the silk has retained its beautiful sheen.

Dyed silk

Merino wool

50% silk/50% wool blend

25% Alpaca/75% Wool

These blends were made using Corriedale wool and alpaca. The batts felt much softer than pure wool, even with as little as 25% Alpaca. As the alpaca roving was well carded, it only took one pass for these blends to be carded enough for spinning. The second blend uses two colours with the alpaca which gives it an interesting streaky look.

Wool   *Wool*

Alpaca

Alpaca blended with one colour

Alpaca blended with two colours

40% Alpaca/60% Wool

This blend uses a combination of natural colours and dyed sliver. The alpaca and natural grey looked a little dull on their own so I added a dash of Corriedale "Nutmeg" to spice up the blend. It feels very soft.

Alpaca

Corriedale, natural grey

Corriedale wool sliver, "Nutmeg"

Alpaca/wool blend

40% Mohair/60% Wool

Use at least 30-40% mohair in a wool/mohair blend to retain the lustre of the mohair. This blend feels fluffy and soft.

Mohair-wool blend

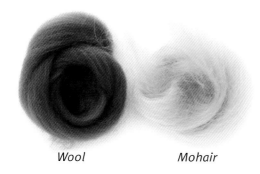

Wool   *Mohair*

10% Angora/50% silk/40% Wool

Angora fibres are usually very short and quite difficult to spin on their own. Blending with wool makes spinning a breeze. Merino wool was used in this lovely blend.

Angora/silk/wool blend

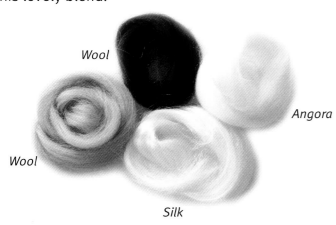

Wool

Wool

Silk

Angora

Colour

Colour Theory

For some people, using colour in their fibre work comes naturally but it is probably fair to say that most fibre artists will have studied colour at some point whilst learning their craft. There are many sources of inspiration for using colour. Some people like the safety of the colour wheel and the reliable harmonies it provides whereas others like to use their instincts and surroundings. Fabrics, artwork, magazines, photographs and nature all provide inspiration. Keep a notebook handy to jot down ideas or start a scrapbook for magazine cuttings and photographs. Once you start looking at your surroundings as possible colour blends, you won't be able to stop.

The colour wheel has 12 colour families, each one with an infinite number of tints, tones and shades. Learning about basic colour theory and the harmonies of the colour wheel provides you with an effective means of choosing colours for successful blends. These harmonies or 'recipes' are by no means hard and fast rules which you must adhere to, but rather a guide to get you going and whet your appetite for your own magical mixes. Playing with colour is by far the best way to learn.

This section looks at basic colour theory and gives examples of different ways to use colour harmonies. I used the drum carder to make the samples shown, however, you can obtain similar results with a set of hand carders.

The 12 hues of the colour wheel

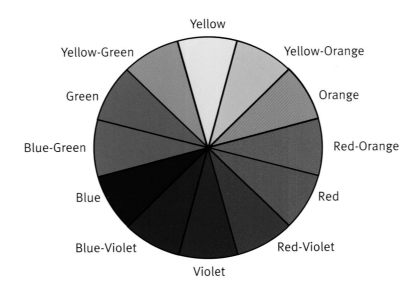

Describing Colour

Hue
A wedge of colour on the colour wheel. Can be called Hue Family or Colour Family. Can be any variation within that family.

Saturation
Intensity/vibrancy of a colour.

Value
Lightness or darkness of a colour.

Colour Harmonies

Primary Colours
Red, yellow and blue are the three primary colours from which all other colours are made.

Secondary Colours
When two primary colours are mixed together they form a secondary colour:

Yellow + Blue = Green
Blue + Red   = Violet
Red + Yellow   = Orange

Tertiary Colours
When one primary colour and its adjacent secondary colour are mixed together they form a tertiary colour:

Yellow + Orange = Yellow-Orange
Yellow + Green   = Yellow-Green
Blue + Green   = Blue-Green
Blue + Violet   = Blue-Violet
Red + Violet   = Red-Violet
Red + Orange   = Red-Orange

Complementary Colours
Lie directly opposite each other on the colour wheel.

46

Analogous Colours	Found close together on the colour wheel, usually within one quarter of the wheel.
Warm/Cool Colours	One half of the colour wheel has warm colours and the other half cool:
	Warm: Yellow-green through orange to red inclusive Cool: Red-Violet through blue to green inclusive
Tints, Tones and Shades	White + colour = tint Grey + colour = tone Black + colour = shade
Neutrals	Black, white, greys and browns.
Monochromatic Colours	Mono = one, Chroma - colour Monochromatic colours are the various tints, tones and shades of a particular hue.

Primary Colours

The colour wheel has three primary colours - yellow, red, blue - from which all other colours are mixed. The following examples show variations of the primary colours using different values and saturations of each hue. I used the Ashford range of Corriedale sliver for these exercises.

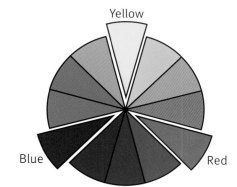

Yellow

Blue

Red

Three bright or highly saturated primary colours

Red

Blue

Yellow

Three primary colours colours light in value

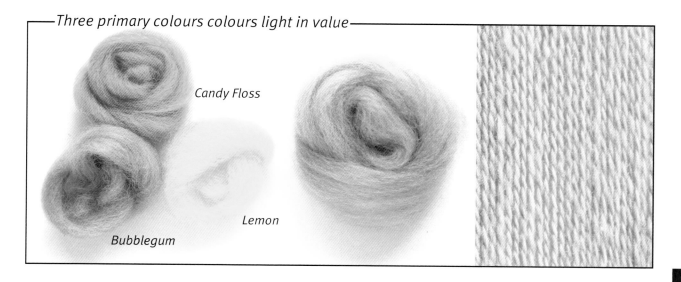

Candy Floss

Lemon

Bubblegum

48

— Three primary colours medium in value —

Lagoon

Pansy

Lemon

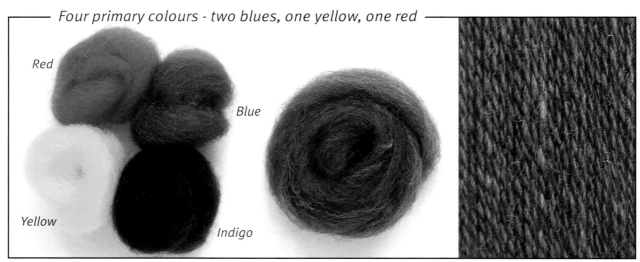

— Four primary colours - two blues, one yellow, one red —

Red

Blue

Yellow

Indigo

 You can use any shade in any proportion of each colour

Secondary Colours

When two primary colours are mixed together, they create a secondary colour:

Yellow + Blue = Green
Blue + Red   = Violet
Red + Yellow = Orange

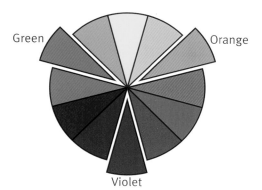

Using several colours in one blend is exciting but the number of passes through the carder will have an effect on how distinct each colour remains. Each pass reduces the clarity of each colour and if there are too many passes, eventually the blend becomes muddy and dull. These three examples show the difference between one, two and three passes.

Each yarn comprises the same six colours in equal amounts, two from each hue, carded in layers.

Purple   Grape Jelly   Tangerine   Orange   Bean Sprout   Green

One pass   *Two passes*   *Three passes*

A layered blend comprising three hues spaced equally on the colour wheel can sometimes become a little dull. By using a higher proportion of one of the hues, you can create a dominant look. Think of this as a recipe - for example - one part of this, two parts of that.

Green Dominant

3 parts green
2 parts violet
1 part orange

Kiwifruit, Green, Bean Sprout, Purple, Grape Jelly, Orange

Violet Dominant

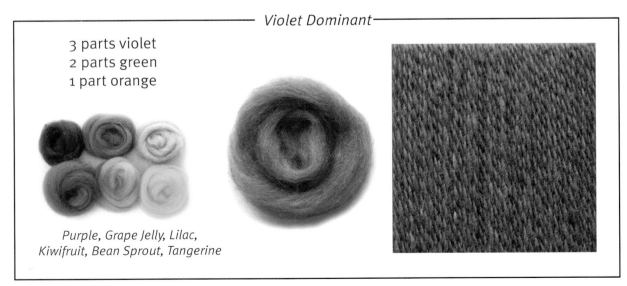

3 parts violet
2 parts green
1 part orange

Purple, Grape Jelly, Lilac, Kiwifruit, Bean Sprout, Tangerine

Orange Dominant

3 parts orange
2 parts green
1 part violet

*Tangerine, Orange, Pumpkin Pie
Kiwifruit, Bean Sprout, Grape Jelly*

 Making a dominant look in a blend works well using Primary colours

Tertiary Colours

When a secondary colour and its adjacent primary are mixed, they create a tertiary colour. You can make exciting and rich blends because you get to use a minimum of six colours, every second colour on the wheel.

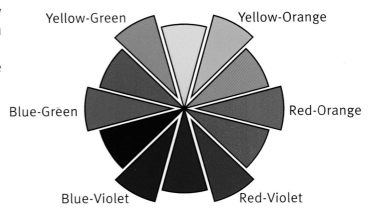

Primary + Secondary = Tertiary

Blue	+ Violet	= Blue-Violet
Blue	+ Green	= Blue-Green
Yellow	+ Green	= Yellow-Green
Yellow	+ Orange	= Yellow-Orange
Red	+ Orange	= Red-Orange
Red	+ Violet	= Red-Violet

As you learned in 'Blending Colours Side-by-Side', the more colours you use in a blend, the less vibrant each one will be. The way you spin and ply multi-coloured blends will also affect how clear and bright each colour remains. A thick yarn will show larger areas of each colour than a finely spun yarn. For each of these exercises I used these six colours:

Magenta   Blueberry Pie   Turquoise   Bean Sprout   Tangerine   Chilli Pepper

2-ply yarn spun fine

2-ply yarn spun thick

You can keep colours clear and bright by plying a single of cool colours with a single of warm colours:

Cool Blend
Turquoise, Magenta, Blueberry Pie

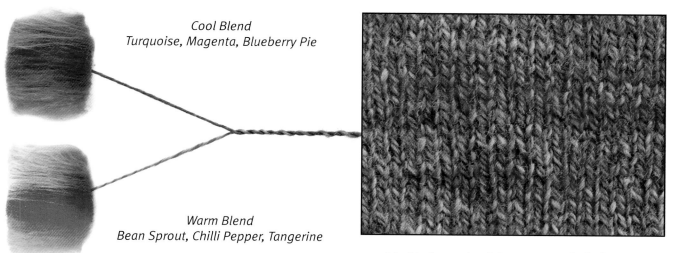

Warm Blend
Bean Sprout, Chilli Pepper, Tangerine

A knitted sample of the warm-cool plied yarn

In multi-coloured blends, cool colours recede and warm colours come forward

Complementary Colours

Complementary colours use two hues that lie directly opposite each other on the colour wheel. When a colour is blended with its complement, the colours become duller so take care with this harmony that you don't overblend.

I only had to step out into the garden to be inspired by nature's perfection at using this harmony. I chose three pairs of complementary colours and made two different samples for each pair, using the same set of colours. Placing the colours side-by-side on the carder kept the colours clear and distinct throughout the yarn. Blending in layers dulled them down and they are much less vibrant.

Red/Green

Chilli Pepper

Green Tea

Lime

Nutmeg

Kiwi Fruit

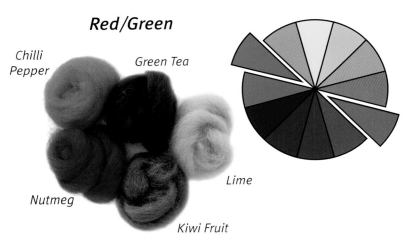

Two reds and three greens were chosen from the Corriedale colour range for a wonderful complementary mix

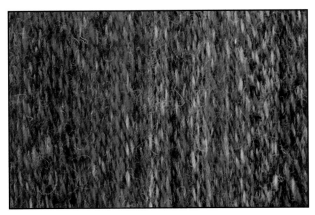

Carded side-by-side

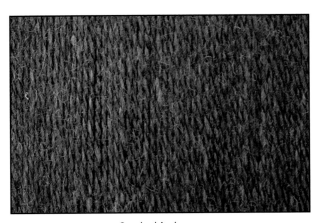

Carded in layers

Yellow/Violet

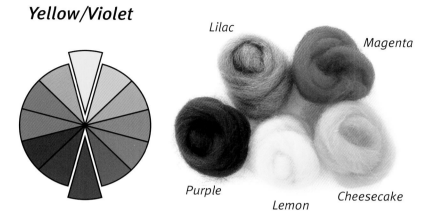

This yellow/violet blend was inspired by this pansy. I used two shades of violet, two yellows and a splash of 'Magenta'.

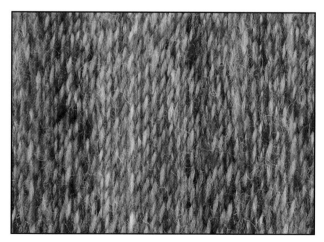

Carded side-by-side

Carded in layers

Blue/Orange

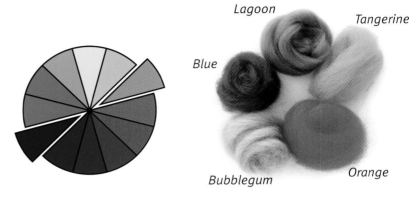

Lagoon

Tangerine

Blue

Bubblegum

Orange

My favourite flower in the garden, the 'Himalayan Poppy', has the perfect shades of orange and blue for a complementary blend.

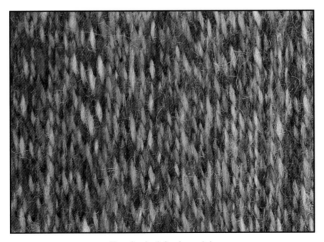

Carded side-by-side

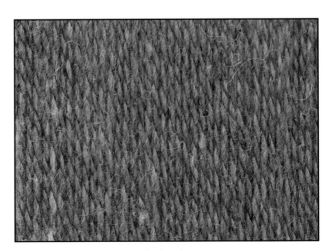

Carded in layers

Analogous Colours

Analogous colours are those which are close to each other on the colour wheel, usually including three hues. Because analogous colours are closely related, they often blend into what appears to be a new solid colour. You can make more interesting blends by using a variety of colour values. For these exercise I used the Ashford range of coloured Corriedale sliver.

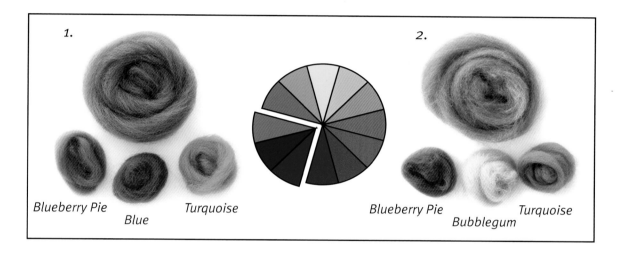

1.
Blueberry Pie
Blue
Turquoise

2.
Blueberry Pie
Bubblegum
Turquoise

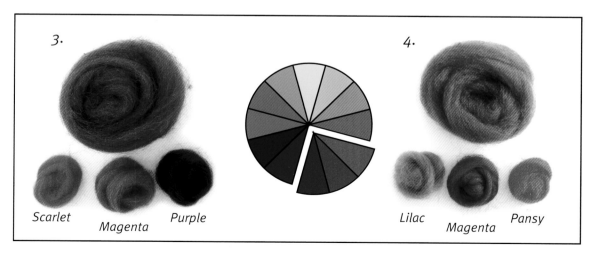

3.
Scarlet
Magenta
Purple

4.
Lilac
Magenta
Pansy

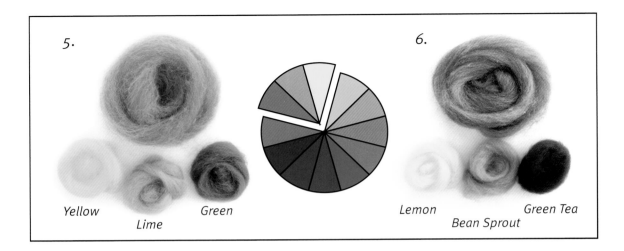

5. Yellow Lime Green

6. Lemon Bean Sprout Green Tea

You can have some fun with analogous colours by spinning singles from two different blends and plying them together. These examples of 2-ply yarns were made using 4 of the blends shown above:

1. Plied with 2

1. Plied with 3

3. Plied with 5

Colour Variations

Sometimes the colour we imagine for a blend doesn't quite work. Maybe it needs to be lighter, darker, warmer or cooler. You can tweak your blend to suit your intended yarn.

Warm/Cool Colours

Colours can be described as a warm or cool:

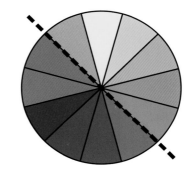

Warm: Yellow-green through orange to red inclusive
Cool: Red-Violet through blue to green inclusive

Make a colour warmer by blending in any colour from the warm half of the colour wheel.

Make a colour cooler by blending in any colour from the cool half of the colour wheel.

'Pansy" plus 'Tangerine' for a warmer colour

'Pansy' plus 'Blueberry Pie' for a cooler colour

Tints, Tones and Shades

Colour values (light/dark) can be described as tints, tones or shade. Adding white makes a tint, adding grey makes a tone and adding black makes a shade.

Original Colour
'Lagoon'

Add white to make a tint.
Makes a colour lighter.

Add grey to make a tone.
Makes a colour duller.

Add black to make a shade.
Makes a colour darker.

 Try using the natural colours of different fibres to make tints, tones, and shades - white silk, grey fleece or black alpaca

Projects

Self-striping Socks

Fun socks to knit in five
gorgeous Corriedale colours

Warm Mittens for Cool Days

A layered blend of warm and
cool colours in toasty warm Merino

Gull-wing Shawl

Quick and easy to knit
in garter stitch

Merino/Silk Scarf
Soft, subtle and luxurious

Self-striping Socks

Self-striping Socks

I prefer to knit socks with a self-striping yarn rather than join in a new colour every two or three rounds. It's fun watching the colours emerge as you knit which makes it hard to put the knitting down and the socks are sure to get finished. I made a 2-ply yarn comprising one self-striping single and the other a blend of all five colours used.

Project Materials:

1 set of double pointed knitting needles:
Metric size 3.25mm, US size 3, UK/Can size 10

Ashford Corriedale Sliver:
1 oz (28 grams) each of:
Lagoon, Pumpkin Pie, Pansy, Tangerine, Magenta or five colours of your choice.

Gauge: 7 sts = 1 inch (2.5 cm)
Size: Woman's medium

Divide each colour in half to make two groups of five colours. One group will be used to make two self-striping batts and the other group will make two blended batts.

Take one set of colours and make the self-striping batts as follows:

Step 1
Using "Lagoon", feed a thin layer across the width of the drum.

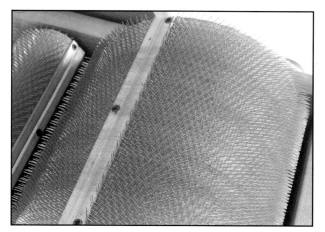

Thin layer of Lagoon on the drum

Step 2
Use the other four colours to make short stripes around the drum. You can place them on in any order you like.

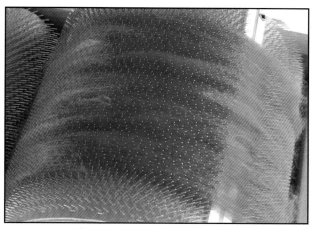

Short stripes around the drum

Step 3
Feed on another thin layer of "Lagoon" as you did in Step 1. The stripes will now be sandwiched between the two thin layers.

Step 4
Carefully remove the batt and divide lengthwise into three equal strips for spinning.

Self-striping batt split into three strips

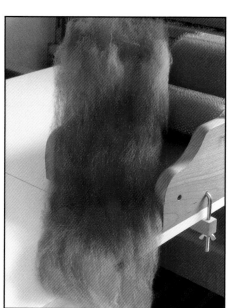

Self-striping batt

Step 6

With the second group of colours, make two layered batts using half of each colour in each batt. Pass twice through the carder. Spin to the same thickness as the striped single.

Five colour blend

Step 7

Ply your two singles together and wash before knitting.

To Knit The Socks

Abbreviations:

k	knit
p	purl
st(s)	stitch(es)
sl1	slip one knitwise
psso	pass slip stitch over
k2tog	knit two together
p2tog	purl two together

Cast on 48 sts loosely (16 sts on needles 1, 2 and 3) and work 10 rounds in k1, p1 rib then knit all rounds until sock measures 8 inches (20 cm) including the ribbing.

Heel Flap:

K the 16 sts on needle 1 and 8 sts from needle 2 onto the same needle. Turn and purl back on these 24 sts. With the first 24 sts, work 17 rows in stocking stitch (knit 1 row, purl 1 row).

Turning the Heel:

Next Row: P15, p2tog, turn
Next Row: K7, sl1, k1, psso, turn
Next Row: P7, p2tog, turn

Repeat the last two rows until 9 sts remain then turn and k7, sl1, k1, psso.

Heel Shaping:

Needle 1:	Pick up and k 19 sts along the first side of the heel.
Needle 2:	Knit across the 24 sts from needles 2 and 3.
Needle 3:	Pick up and k 19 sts along the other side of the heel.

You should now have 70 sts on four needles.

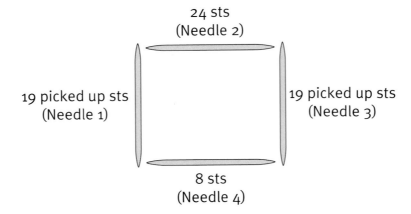

24 sts
(Needle 2)

19 picked up sts
(Needle 1)

19 picked up sts
(Needle 3)

8 sts
(Needle 4)

Re-arrange the stitches onto three needles by slipping 4 sts from needle 4 onto needle 1 and the remaining 4 sts on needle 4 onto needle 3.

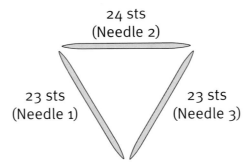

24 sts
(Needle 2)

23 sts
(Needle 1)

23 sts
(Needle 3)

Decrease Round:

Needle 1:   Knit to last 3 sts, k2tog, k1
Needle 2:   Knit across the 24 stitches
Needle 3:   K1, sl1, k1, psso, knit to end

Knit one round with shaping

Repeat the last two rounds until you have a total of 48 sts, 12 sts on needle 1, 24 sts on needle 2 and 12 sts on needle 3.

Foot Length:

Knit 30 rounds or until the total foot length from the heel shaping is 2 inches (5 cm) shorter than the length of your foot.

Toe Shaping

Decrease Round:	Needle 1:	Knit to last 3 sts, k2tog, k1
	Needle 2:	K1, sl1, k1, psso, knit to last 3 sts, k2tog, k1
	Needle 3:	K1, sl1, k1, psso, knit to end
Next Round:	Knit	

Repeat the last two rounds until there are 24 sts then work two decrease rounds - 16 sts remain. With needle 3, knit across the 4 sts on needle 1. You now have 2 needles each with 8 sts.

Break the yarn leaving a tail of 8 inches (20cm). Thread through a blunt needle and graft the two sets of sts together. Thread the yarn through to the back and weave into the knitting.

Neaten the top edge of each sock if necessary and weave in the end.

Warm Mittens for Cool Days

Warm Mittens for Cool Days

These Merino mittens are quick and easy to knit and will keep your hands toasty warm on cold winter mornings. Three colours are warm and three are cool making a rich, heathered yarn.

Project Materials:

1 set double pointed knitting needles:
Metric size 4 mm, US size 6, UK size 8

Ashford Merino Sliver
½ oz (14 grams) each of:
Scarlet, Tangerine, Raspberry, Blueberry Pie,
Spearmint, Green Tea

Size: To fit woman's average hand
Gauge: 6 sts = 1 inch (2.5 cm)

Carding and Spinning

Divide each colour into four equal portions, making four groups of six colours. Use each group to make a layered blend, making two passes through the carder. Pull each batt in a sliver.

Spin two slivers onto one bobbin and two onto another and ply together. Wash the yarn in warm water with a liquid wool wash.

To Knit the Mittens

Abbreviations:
k	knit
p	purl
st(s)	stitch(es)
sl1	slip one knitwise
k2tog	knit two together
m1	make one

Cast on 42 sts, dividing them evenly onto three needles. Work 15 rounds of K2, P2 rib. Change to stocking stitch.

Next round: K7, m1, k14, m1, k14, m1, k7 (45 sts).
Knit 3 rounds.

Thumb Shaping

Stitches for the thumb are made by making a gusset. An increase is made each side of the centre stitch(es) on every second round:

Round 1:   K22, m1, k1, m1, k22 (47 sts)
Round 2:   Knit
Round 3:   K22, m1, k3, m1, k22 (49 sts)
Round 4:   Knit
Round 5:   K22, m1, k5, m1, k22 (51 sts)
Round 6:   Knit

Continue increasing in this way until there are 15 stitches between the two increases. You should now have a total of 59 sts - 15 on needle 1, 29 on needle 2 and 15 on needle 3.

Next Row: K22, place the next 15 sts (thumb stitches) on a length of yarn, m1, knit to end (45 sts). The m1 in this row replaces the centre stitch used in the thumb gusset.

Continue in stocking stitch until mitten measures approximately 7.5 inches (19 cm) or reaches the top of your little finger.

Next round: (Knit 13, k2tog) three times - 42 sts

Shape Top

Round 1:   (K12, k2tog) three times - 39 sts
Round 2:   Knit
Round 3:   (K11, k2tog) three times - 36 sts
Round 4:   Knit

Continue decreasing every other round in this way, working 1 less st between decreases, until 27 sts remain.

Now decrease every round until 6 sts remain. Break off yarn, thread through sts and pull tight. Weave in on the wrong wide.

Thumb

Place the 15 thumb sts evenly onto three needles and knit all rounds until thumb measures to the middle of your thumbnail.

Next Round: (K3, k2tog) 3 times
Next Round: Knit
Next Round: (K2 k2tog) 3 times
Next Round: Knit
Next Round: (K1 k2tog) 3 times
Next Round: Knit

Break off yarn, thread through the remaining 6 sts and pull tight. Weave in thread on the wrong side.

Gull-wing Shawl

Gull-wing Shawl

This is an easy to knit shawl and can be worn in several different ways. I decided to add some sparkle to the shawl by using a multi-coloured rayon sliver I picked up at a fibre fair. If you don't have any multi-coloured sliver, increase the amount of each Corriedale colour to 2½ oz (70 grams).

Project Materials:

Circular knitting needle   Metric size 6mm
                                            US size 10
                                            UK/Can size 4

2 oz (56 grams) each of:
Cookie, Chilli Pepper, Green Tea, Pumpkin Pie

2 oz (56 grams) of nylon or wool multi-coloured sliver

Carding and Spinning

Pull off 10 inch (25 cm) lengths from each Corriedale colour and the multi-coloured sliver. Use one length from each colour to make a layered batt. Pass through the carder 2 times. Pull each batt into a sliver ready for spinning.

Spin into fine singles using an even number of bobbins ready for making a 2-ply yarn.

The blend

The yarn

Shawl Pattern

Abbreviations:

k	knit
st(s)	stitch(es)
yo	yarn over

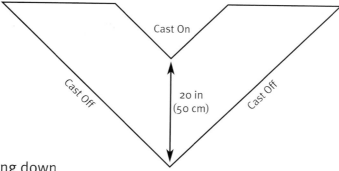

You are starting from the neck and knitting down.

Cast on 71 sts very loosely using the long-tail cast on method.

Row 1: Knit.
Row 2: K2, yo, knit to centre stitch, yo, k1, yo, knit to last two sts, yo, k2

Repeat these two rows until the shawl measures 20 inches (50 cm) down the centre.

Cast off loosely.

Making the fringe:

Use 3 x 12 inch (30 cm) strands of yarn for each tassle. Beginning at the first stitch on the cast-on edge, secure each tassle with a hitch knot by drawing the centre of the strands through the stitch forming a loop. Take the ends of the strands through the loop and pull firmly.

Make a tassle for every third stitch along the cast-on edge.

Wash the shawl in lukewarm water with a mild detergent or wool wash. Roll loosely in a towel and squeeze gently to remove excess water, or use the spin cycle on your washing machine. Lay flat to dry.

Pattern by Mary Knox

Soft and Subtle
Merino/Silk Scarf

Soft and Subtle - Merino/Silk Scarf

Several of my fellow spinners have recently knitted scarves lengthwise by casting on lots of stitches and knitting each row with a different colour. It's a great way to use up small amounts of yarn left over from other projects. I thought this idea would also work well using a variegated yarn which I could create by making a layered blend on the drum carder.

I had a small quantity of dyed silk in bright primary colours in my cupboard which I decided would be lovely blended with white Merino for a soft, warm scarf in subtle colours. I plied my handspun yarn with a fine commercial silk yarn.

Project Materials:

Knitting needles:
Metric size 4 mm and 4.5mm,
US size 6 and 7, UK/Can size 7 and 8

Dyed silk in primary colours or three colours of your choice - total weight ½ oz (14 grams). Use the same proportion for each colour.

½ oz (14 grams) of Ashford white Merino sliver

250 yards (228 metres) of white 10/2 silk yarn.

If you don't have any dyed silk, use white silk and choose three colours from the Ashford Merino sliver range.

Carding and Spinning

Blend each colour of the silk with an equal quantity of white Merino using the fibre blending technique described on page 39. I passed each batt through the carder 3 times to create a tint of each silk colour.

Divide each batt in half lengthwise. Take one half of each of the blended batts and make a layered blend, passing the fibre through the carder just the once. Primary colours are inclined to look dull if they are overblended.

Make a second layered batt using the other half of the blended batts.

Pull into a thin sliver, letting the colours come and go as they please. This will give a lovely variegated look in the spinning and create subtle areas of secondary colours where there were blends of two primaries.

Spin a fine single and ply with the commercial silk thread.

To Knit the Scarf

Using the larger needles, cast on 200 stitches leaving a tail of 6 inches (15 cm).
Change to smaller needles and knit garter stitch for 29 rows.
Change to larger needles and cast off very loosely.

To Make the Twisted Fringe

Cut 60 x 10 inch (25 cm) lengths of the plied yarn.

Step 1.

Using a blunt tapestry needle, thread 2 lengths through the loop on the end of the first row, pulling them through to half their length. You now have 4 threads hanging from the loop.

Step 2.

Take 2 ends and twist them in the opposite direction to the plying - about 10-12 twists. Secure between two fingers of one hand, and twist the other two threads the same way with your other hand.

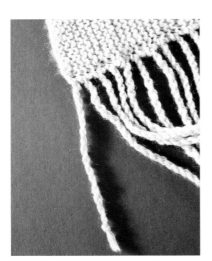

Step 3.

Now bring the two twisted ends together and twist in the opposite direction for 10-12 twists. Secure near the ends with an overhand knot.

Work across the end of the scarf, threading two lengths of yarn into every second loop.

Wash in warm water with a few drops of liquid detergent. Lay flat to dry.

Sampling

I am an avid sampler. In the early years of my carding and spinning, I didn't bother making samples and as a result there were disappointments. Now I make samples for every yarn and can confidently begin a project knowing that the blend of colours or fibres are exactly what I imagined. Making samples is also a great way to learn about colour and fibre blends. Just a few staples of fleece or sliver are enough to make enough yarn to either wrap around a piece of cardboard for future reference or knit up. You can quickly blend together a few different colours with hand carders or use the drum carder for special techniques such as self-striping batts. Handspun yarn invariably changes after washing so take time to do this too.

Keep a notebook handy so you can record colours, proportions, fibres and how you carded, spun and plied your fibre. These records are invaluable, not only for your current project, but for future projects. Store them in an organised fashion for easy reference. I like to use self-sealing plastic bags in which I keep a small amount of each fibre, a sample of the resulting blend and the spun yarn wrapped around a stiff piece of cardboard.

When making a sample of 2-ply yarn, I find it easier to spin the fibre onto one bobbin and ply it from my hand rather than spinning it onto two bobbins for plying.

How to ply from your hand using the Andean method:

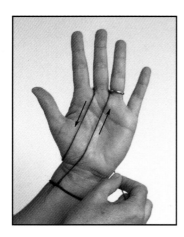

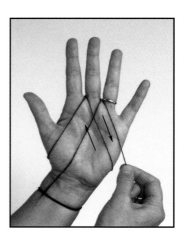

Step 1

First, secure the end of the yarn by tucking it into your cuff, watch strap or a rubber band. Take the yarn up and behind your middle finger, then down and around the back of your hand.

Step 2

Now bring the yarn up and behind your middle finger, then down and around the back of your hand in the opposite direction to Step 1.

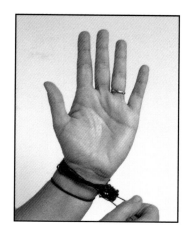

Step 3

Repeat Steps 1 and 2 until all the yarn is wound on to your hand. Keeping both ends together, slip the yarn off your middle finger to form a 'bracelet' around your wrist.

Step 4

Attach the ends to your bobbin leader, and you are now ready to ply.

The Ashford mini niddy-noddy is perfect for winding hand-plied yarn into a small hank.

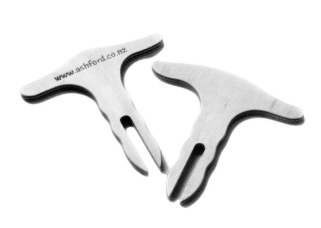

Glossary

Awl/Doffer	A long, pointed metal tool used to separate fibres for removal from a drum carder.
Batt	A rectangle of fibre that has been prepared by a drum carder.
Doffing Strip	Metal strip across the large drum of a drum carder where the fibre is separated for removal.
Carding Cloth	A piece of leather or rubber material fitted with rows of metal teeth and attached to carding tools.
Combed Top	A rope-like bundle of fibre of consistent thickness that has been finely combed to remove short fibres and aligns the remaining long fibres in a parallel arrangement for worsted spinning.
Crimp	The natural wave in staples of wool fibre.
Fleece	The wool from a single sheep.
Hue	A wedge of colour from the colour wheel.
Navajo Plying	A method of making a 3-ply yarn from an unplied yarn.
Rolag	A small roll of fibre that is the result of carding with hand carders.
Single	An unplied yarn.
Sliver	A continuous length of carded fibre.
Staple	The length of a lock of shorn wool.
Worsted	Smooth yarn spun from long staples of combed fibre.

The Ashford sliver comes in Corriedale, Merino or Alpaca-wool blend.
Colours are updated regularly - check out the latest on www.ashford.co.nz

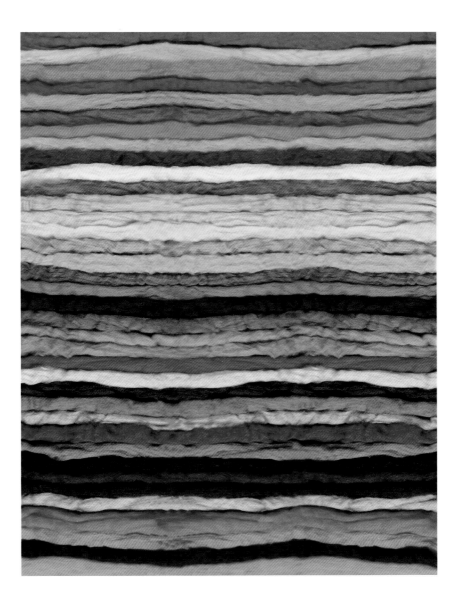

The Ashford carding tools and fibres used in this book are available around the world.
For the name of your nearest store contact one of the distributors below.

NEW ZEALAND:
Ashford Handicrafts Limited
PO Box 474, Ashburton
Tel: (+64-3) 308 9087
Fax: (+64-3) 308 8664
email: sales@ashford.co.nz
www.ashford.co.nz

AUSTRALIA:
Ashford Australia Pty Limited
Cooma, NSW
Tel:(+61-2) 64524422
FreePh:(1800)026397
Fax: (+61-2) 64524523
email: ashford@snowy.net.au
www.ashfordaustralia.com

AUSTRIA:
Wiener Webwaren
Vienna
Tel: (+43-1) 292 7108
email: info@wienerwebwaren.at
www.wienerwebwaren.at

CANADA:
Harmonique Spinning Wheels &
Looms
Victoria, BC
Tel:(+1-250) 294 4411
Fax:(+1-250) 294 8411
email: info@harmonique.ca
www.harmonique.ca

CHILE:
Sociedad Commercial Wisniak
Santiago
Tel: (+56-2) 5569221
Fax: (+56-2) 5516519
email: losalata@interaccess.cl
www.costuritas.cl

CZECH REPUBLIC:
Dalin Praha Sro
Praha
Tel: (+420-2) 74860304
Fax: (+420-2) 74860304
email: dlinhartova@dalin-praha.cz
www.dalin-praha.cz

DENMARK:
Skytten
4871 Horbelev
Tel:(+45) 5444 5020
Fax:(+45) 5444 5022
email:mail@skytten-danmark.dk

Spindelvaeven
5800 Nyborg
Tel:(+45) 6611 1499
email: vibe@spindelvaeven.dk
www.spindelvaeven.dk

FRANCE:
Ets P Marie Saint Germain
Remiremont, Cedex
Tel:(+33 3) 29 23 00 48
Fax:(+33 3) 29 23 20 70
email: contact@artifilum.com
www.artifilum.com

GERMANY:
Monika Traub
Winterbach
Tel:(+49-7181) 70910
Fax:(+49-7181) 709111
email: moni@traub-wolle.de
www.traub-wolle.de

HOLLAND:
The Spinners
Den Haag
Tel:(+31-7) 0397 3643
email: boer381@zonnet.nl
www.despinners.nl

JAPAN:
Ananda Co Limited
Yamanashi
Tel:(+81-551) 32 4215
Fax:(+81-551) 32 4830
email: wool@ananda.jp
www.ananda.jp

Craft Hitsujiza
Fukuoka-shi
Tel:(+81-92) 8511 358
Fax:(+81-92) 8511 358

Mariya Handicrafts Limited
Sapporo
Tel:(+81-11) 221 3307
Fax:(+81-11) 232 0393
email: koichi-m@ra2.so-net.ne.jp

Ocean Trading Co Ltd
Kyoto
Tel:(+81-75) 314 8720
Fax:(+81-75) 313 6150
email: green@oceantrading.co.jp
www.oceantrading.co.jp/spinning

Sanyo Trading Company Limited
Ibaraki
Tel:(+81) 297 78 1000
Fax:(+81) 297 78 5850
email: adx01490@ams.odn.ne.jp

MALAYSIA:
Multifilla (M) Sdn BHD
Selangor Darul Ehsan
Tel: (+60-3) 89613686
Fax: (+60-3) 89613637
email: mfilla@tm.net.my
www.multifilla.com

NORWAY:
Spinninger
Billingstad
Tel:(+47) 66 84 60 22
Fax:(+47) 66 84 60 22

REPUBLIC OF KOREA:
LDH Hand Weaving Loom
Fine Corp Ltd
Seoul
Tel:(+82-2) 779 1894
Fax:(+82-2) 755 1663
email: finecenter@finecenter.com
www.finecenter.com

SOUTH AFRICA:
Campbell Crafts & Marketing
Cape Town
Tel:(+27) 21-686 6668
Fax:(+27) 21-448 8506
email: campbellcrafts@netactive.co.za

SWEDEN:
Gudruns Ullbod
Enkoping
Tel:(+46-171) 399 95
Fax:(+46-171) 399 96
email: ullbod@gudrunsullbod.com

SWITZERLAND:
Spycher-Handwerk
Huttwil
Tel:(+41-629) 62 1152
Fax:(+41-629) 62 1160
email: info@spycher-handwerk.ch
www.spycher-handwerk.ch

TAIWAN:
Founder Tek Int'l Co Ltd
Taipei
Tel:(+886-2) 2-781 1699
Fax:(+886-2) 2-751 2521
email: foundtwn@ms12.hinet.net
www.foundertek.com.tw

UNITED KINGDOM:
Haldanes Craft and Tools Ltd
Fife
Tel:(+44-1383) 821406
Fax:(+44-1383) 825331
email: haldanesLTD@aol.com
www.haldanes.co.uk

UNITED STATES:
Foxglove Fiberarts Supply
Bainbridge Island, Washington
Tel:(+1-206) 780-2747
Fax:(+1-206) 780-2848
email: sales@foxglovefiber.com
www.foxglovefiber.com

Other Ashford books available

The Ashford Book of
Weaving for the Four Shaft Loom
By Anne Field
ISBN: 1-8774270-1-2

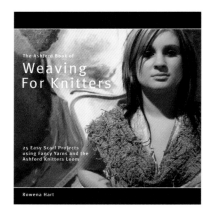

The Ashford Book of
Weaving for Knitters
By Rowena Hart
ISBN: 0-9582631-5-9

The Ashford Book of
Dyeing
By Ann Milner
ISBN: 1-8774271-4-4

The Ashford Book of
Projects for the Eight
Shaft Loom
By Elsa Krogh
ISBN: 0-9582631-4-0

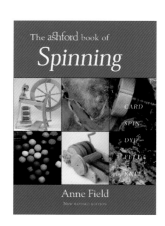

The Ashford Book of
Spinning
By Anne Field
ISBN: 0-9087049-4-1

The Ashford Book of
Rigid Heddle Weaving
By Rowena Hart
ISBN: 0-4730843-7-6

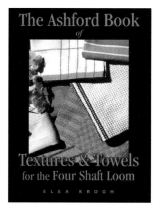

The Ashford Book of
Textures & Towels
By Elsa Krogh
ISBN: 1-8772511-5-1